W9-BIL-361

5-20-95   5.30

GRAMERCY GREAT MASTERS

Rembrandt van Rijn

Gramercy Books
New York • Avenel

Acknowledgments
The publishers would like to thank the museums for reproduction permission and in particular the **BRIDGEMAN ART LIBRARY** for their help in supplying the illustrations for the book.

Aurora Trust: Abraham Serving the Three Angels.
Christie's, London: Soldier in a Plumed Hat.
Dahlem Staatliche Gemaldegalerie, Berlin: Moses with the Tablets of the Law.
Galleria degli Uffizi, Florence: Self-Portrait with Gorget and Beret.
Gemaldegalerie, Kassel: Winter Landscape with Skaters; Jacob Blessing the Sons of Joseph.
Gemaldegalerie, Berlin: The Man with the Golden Helmet.
Glasgow Art Gallery and Museum: The Slaughtered Ox; Alexander the Great.
Hermitage, St. Petersburg: Saskia as Flora; The Descent from the Cross; The Angel Preventing Abraham from Sacrificing His Son Isaac; Danaë, or Aegina Visited by Jupiter in the Form of Fire; Haman Recognizes His Fate; The Return of the Prodigal Son.
Louvre, Paris: Scholar in Meditation; The Holy Family; Christ at Emmaus.
Mauritshuis, The Hague: Self-Portrait with Gorget; The Anatomy Lesson of Dr. Tulp; An Officer; Susannah Surprised by the Elders; Portrait of a Bareheaded Man; Two Negroes; Homer; Self-Portrait Laughing.
Minneapolis Society of Fine Arts: The Suicide of Lucretia.
Pushkin Museum, Moscow: Portrait of an Old Woman in a Veil.
National Gallery, London: Peter and Paul in Conversation; Christ and the Woman Taken in Adultery; The Adoration of the Shepherds; A Woman Bathing.
National Gallery of Scotland, Edinburgh: Sarah Waiting for Tobias.
National Museum of Wales, Cardiff: Portrait of Catrina Hooghsaet.
National Museum of Stockholm: Simeon's Song of Praise.
Prado, Madrid: Artemisia Receiving Her Husband's Ashes Mixed with Wine.
Private collections: Soldier with Sword; Female Figure with Laurel Crown; Portrait of Saskia with a Hat; An Old Woman Reading.
Rijksmuseum-Stichting, Amsterdam: The Night Watch.
Staatliche Kunstammlungen, Dresden: Rembrandt and Saskia in the Scene: The Prodigal Son in a Bordello.
Victoria and Albert Museum, London: The Departure of the Sunamitic Woman.
Walter Hussey Bequest Pallant House, Chichester: The Flight into Egypt.

Copyright © 1993 I Dioscuri, Genova
Copyrigt © 1993 Craig Hill Italia, Genova
Copyrigt © 1994 by Outlet Book Company, Inc.
All rights reserved

This 1994 edition is published by Gramercy Books,
distributed by Outlet Book Company, Inc.
a Random House Company,
40 Engelhard Avenue
Avenel, New Jersey 07001

Printed and bound in Italy

8 7 6 5 4 3 2 1

Rembrandt van Rijn
His Life and Works

To think of a Rembrandt painting is to think of light, the inner light of his paintings that makes them glow, that illuminates the soul of his subjects and, ultimately, life itself.

The seventeenth century reflected Rembrandt's style. Throughout Europe, it was considered a golden era, the last great era to be lit by intellectual, spiritual, and artistic thought. The mood was one of great self-satisfaction and certainty.

Holland, the country of the Seven United Netherlandish Provinces, was at the forefront of this golden age of comfort and thought. After years of war with Catholic Spain, truce was declared in 1609. Peace reigned for twelve years, until 1621, but the enterprising merchants of Protestant Holland continued to trade with the enemy despite renewed conflict—and they became considerably wealthier and more powerful.

By the time a peace treaty was signed in 1648, the merchants of Holland, the new middle-class bourgeoisie, had greater opportunities than ever. Industry took its place at the very forefront of progress and change. Money, power, and an excellent quality of life were available for those who had sufficient talent, drive, and business acumen.

The artistic milieu was as active as the merchant guilds. There were plenty of commissions for painters, but the emphasis on

*Jeremiah
Mourns the
Destruction of
Jerusalem* (detail)

industry, on "bourgeoisie" comfort and values, required that the paintings be created along specific, rigid lines. The merchants knew what they wanted and the artists had to comply. Somber representation was key, even if a picture had to lose its perspective, movement, and liveliness to flatter a wealthy merchant's face or to give equal importance to all the members of a guild.

Light was Rembrandt's way out. Light enabled him to work around these rigid rules, overriding the dull, stagnant harmony of contemporary paintings—and still get commissions from his wealthy patrons. Rather than using lighter, brighter colors, Rembrandt made light a tone, turning a corner of a painting golden, making the center of a painting emanate a white glow, as exemplified in *The Night Watch*, his most famous work.

Rembrandt also used light to emphasize details in his paintings, particularly in his early work. Light would emphasize the rivets of a helmet or the sparkle of a ring, as in *Jeremiah Mourns the Destruction of Jerusalem*, providing a focus for the painting's composition and subjects.

Light also created movement. Stagnant, dull, representational portraits were not for Rembrandt. His subjects were faithfully portrayed, but they moved. They were always caught in the process of doing something—be it discussing a business matter, going off to war, or simply staring out from the canvas with provocative emotion.

Light brought Rembrandt's paintings to life; it was part of his genius. Light separated Rembrandt from his contemporaries and made him great—and this is what he aspired to. He not only wanted to paint; he also wanted to be recognized as a great painter. He wanted to express his vision of life—even if it contradicted prevailing beliefs. His lifelong challenge was to illuminate his vision without losing his commissions, without limiting his opportunities to paint and to have his work seen.

Indeed, Rembrandt faced many challenges and obstacles in his life. He would do battle between his artistic vision and his pragmatism, between his creative needs and his need for living well. But, always, his light would not waver. Eventually, in his final years, it would take over. It would become the principal element of his paintings, no longer a function of illumination, but a symbol of his own dreamlike and unapproachable universe, a world that he alone could create, that he alone could master.

EARLY ROOTS

Rembrandt Harmenszoon van Rijn was his full name—Rembrandt, son of Harmen, and van Rijn because the family came from the Rhine River area. He was born in Leiden, Holland, on July 15, 1606. His father, a miller, owned a windmill and was quite prosperous. His mother, Neeltje, was the daughter of a baker. Like other members of the prosperous Dutch bourgeoisie, the van Rijns embraced Calvinism, whose followers, rejecting papal authority, believed the Bible to be the only source of religious truth.

Rembrandt was one of nine children. His brothers were being raised to become businessmen. When Rembrandt was seven years old, his parents sent him to the Latin School of Leiden, probably in the hopes that he would become a lawyer or a clergyman. He studied mathematics, Greek, classical literature, geography, and history, and in 1620, when he was fourteen, he entered Leiden University. The academic setting was liberating. Although a strict Calvinist institution, it was not averse to new ideas, particularly in areas of scientific studies. Anatomy was a favorite course and the anatomy theater at the university was a place of public entertainment. Crowds filled the auditorium, watching, mouths agape, as a cadaver was dissected on stage.

Rembrandt attended these dissections. The knowledge of anatomy he gained and his experience in the anatomy theater proved to be valuable throughout his career. But as much as he enjoyed studying science at the university, Rembrandt's inclinations were more artistic. His strong preference for painting led him to abandon his studies after only a few months, and in 1621, with his father's approval, he became an apprentice to Jacob Van Swanenburgh, a local artist. Swanenburgh had spent time in Italy and it was in his crowded workshop that Rembrandt first learned about the masters of the Italian Renaissance. During his three years as an apprentice, Rembrandt also learned the basic techniques of painting. He studied so diligently and showed such promise that his father sent him to live in Amsterdam for six months.

A VISIT TO AMSTERDAM

Amsterdam was the core of Holland's intellectual, spiritual, and philosophical freedom. Because of its location near a direct route to the North Sea, the city was growing rapidly. It attracted people from within Holland as well as from other countries. Jews persecuted in Spain and Belgians fleeing after the fall of Antwerp were among those who immigrated to Amsterdam, enriching the city with divergent cultures, with exciting new ideas, with sophistication and affluence.

It was an ideal place for an aspiring young artist to learn about the world, and Rembrandt took full advantage. In 1624, he became an apprentice to Pieter Lastman, one of Holland's most celebrated painters of historical scenes. Lastman was also acquainted with the Italian masters. He taught young Rembrandt the subtle art of chiaroscuro, the dramatic light-and-dark shadings that the painter Caravaggio made famous in Italy and which Rembrandt would later take to new, illuminating heights.

But as much as Lastman influenced Rembrandt, the young artist refused to adopt completely his master's pictorial precepts, considering them too formal and stagnant. Indeed, paintings he did of the very same subjects that Lastman had painted were more highly acclaimed. Rembrandt's renditions of historical and biblical scenes were less rhetorical; they had more emotion; they were less sedate. Rembrandt's *Stoning of St. Stephen* and *The Angel and the Prophet Balaam*, for example, were completed during his six-month apprenticeship at Lastman's workshop. Both paintings have a great sense of immediacy and a solidly realistic style with such dramatic effects of chiaroscuro lighting that, even at this early stage, Rembrandt's work stood out from all other depictions of these same themes.

The churches in Calvinist Holland were far less embellished than their Catholic counterparts. Sacred images were eliminated in favor of a spartan atmosphere of spirituality. But, although painters lost the Church as a major source of commissions, they gained an eager and wealthy public. Amsterdam's citizens had an insatiable appetite for religious and historical paintings. The affluent merchant classes had the money to adorn their homes, but their Calvinist values prevented them from ostentatious displays of wealth and possession. Serious, but beautiful, religious and historical paintings were the perfect solutions. And, because they were displayed in homes, these paintings could have a greater freedom of expression and a higher degree of realism than they could on a church wall—where, particularly in non-Protestant countries, realism might be considered almost blasphemous.

By the time Rembrandt was ready to leave Lastman, he already had a following. Never before had anyone seen such expressive, illuminating portrayals of historical and biblical subjects.

RETURN TO LEIDEN

In 1625, Rembrandt returned to Leiden and opened his own studio with a partner, Jan Lievens, a fellow painter and friend from Amsterdam. It was an unusual move. Most aspiring young artists were eager to go to Italy, to see firsthand what they had been studying. But both Rembrandt and Lievens are reported to have said that they didn't want to squander their time "in the bloom of their years traveling to foreign lands. The best Italian works could also be seen outside of Italy."

The paintings the young Rembrandt did in his Leiden studio surpassed those of his master, Lastman, in the chiaroscuro technique. Rather than using chiaroscuro for dramatic effect, as Lastman and his contemporaries did, Rembrandt used it to compose the entire painting. His use of light and dark virtually projected the figures toward the viewer—a technique that would, for the first time, give the viewer a sense of involvement, of emotional and physical attachment to the depicted scene. This technique is obvious in *Christ Purges the Temple*, where the moneychangers seem to seek their escape beyond the confines of the canvas. It is also used to great effect in the 1628 version of *Christ at Emmaus*. In this painting, although strong contrasts of light and shade can be seen, it is difficult to determine exactly where the source of light is; it seems to originate from the very gesture of Christ breaking the bread.

By 1626, Rembrandt had gained a considerable reputation and the Leiden studio was flourishing. *Tobit and Anna* (1626) provides convincing proof that his skills in composition and expression were already developed. In this painting, his ability to ignite a scene with a simple gesture can be seen in the vulnerable, worried posture of the blind old man, as well as in Hannah's resisting and angry stance.

*Self-Portrait
with Gorget*
(detail)

EARLY PORTRAITS

Rembrandt's portraits were in great demand by his Dutch patrons and they formed a considerable part of his work in his Leiden studio. Almost from the start, Rembrandt began collecting costumes and props that would later appear in his portraits. Although he could not yet purchase the original art of the Italian masters, he could collect exotica. He loved fabrics, rich silks, velvets, and lace. He delighted in the detail of gems, belts, necklaces, and rings. He began to collect helmets of brass, old costumes and hats, unused weapons and coins. Rembrandt used these props in his portraits, adorning the sitters with an elaborate necklace, a delicate fan, or perhaps an intricate brass belt buckle.

These accessories accentuated the sitter's personality. Rather than simply producing a faithful likeness, Rembrandt strove toward a new realism. While other portrait painters often enhanced a sitter's appearance for a more pleasing effect, Rembrandt sought the "complex truth concealed within reality." He refused to venerate the sitter. Instead, he used his extraordinary talent to dig deep into the psyche of his subject and to achieve a lively sense of spontaneity.

He also made a point of emphasizing a defect if this helped to define the essential spirit of the sitter. Although some of his patrons were amused by the sardonic quality these portraits might convey, Rembrandt's insistence on realism could also annoy the stolid burghers. Indeed, as Rembrandt grew older and this realism was accentuated in his work, he lost many important and valuable commissions.

Undeterred, Rembrandt went his own way. He even included portraits of friends and members of his family in biblical and historical paintings. *Rembrandt's Mother as the Prophetess Hannah* (1631), for example, shows his mother against a dark background holding an open Bible upon her knees. She is the focal point of the light diffused throughout the picture. Rembrandt's father appears in *Jeremiah Mourns the Destruction of Jerusalem*. And Rembrandt's partner, Lievens, appears in the *Stoning of St. Stephen*, as does Rembrandt himself.

Rembrandt actually appears in almost one hundred of his paintings, engravings, and drawings. His *Self-Portrait with Gorget* (1629-

1630) is considered one of the most significant canvases of his Leiden years. The head of the figure seems to emerge from the greenish-brown background without a specific point of separation. Like condensation, it almost materializes from the atmosphere. The face is a study of variations in tone and shading. The metal collar stands out, enlivened by a ray of light that emphasizes the studs.

Taken together, Rembrandt's self-portraits provide a fascinating pictorial autobiography of the artist, showing him in a variety of vestments and poses, with others and alone, from the days of his youth to his old age. These self-portraits were also an invaluable tool for Rembrandt. Although they display an element of narcissism, they offered him the opportunity to experiment with a wide range of expressions—and they helped him promote himself to his public.

The years in Leiden were productive. In addition to painting historical and biblical scenes and unusual portraits for his wealthy patrons, he also began to experiment with engraving.

ETCHINGS

Rembrandt was fascinated by engraving. With just one etching he could create many copies. His work could be seen by everyone. He enjoyed the etching process, drawing on the copper plate with the sharp burin, and he quickly mastered it.

Rembrandt's earliest engravings, like *The Flight into Egypt* and *The Circumcision*, reflect his experimentation with the process. He used old people, vagabonds, peasants, and paupers in these early etchings, striving for expressive realism in their faces. Rembrandt's later etchings, produced in Leiden in 1630, prove that he had indeed mastered the technique in a remarkably short amount of time. In fact, Rembrandt is unanimously acknowledged by modern critics to have been one of the world's greatest etchers.

From etching to portraiture, biblical paintings to historical scenes, Rembrandt's masterful work in Leiden was profitable. But after his father died in 1630, his family ties became less strong. He felt no need to remain in Leiden. He needed to grow. He needed change. A year later, in 1631, he received a prestigious commission from Amsterdam. Rembrandt decided to move there.

AMSTERDAM: THE FIRST PERIOD

When Dr. Tulp, a well-known physician in Amsterdam, asked Rembrandt to paint him and his assistants at work, the artist set up his studio at the home of his art dealer, Hendrick van Uylenburch. He was pleased to be back. Not only did he have a fine commission, but in Amsterdam there were many wealthy bourgeoisie who were eager to have the famous Rembrandt paint their portraits. Indeed, in his first months in the city, several engravers produced copies of his paintings, not only testifying to his outstanding abilities, but confirming his reputation as well.

Amsterdam's commercial guilds and professional associations liked to have their portraits painted in large, celebrative groups. These were usually portrayed in an unimaginative, stagnant, face-forward fashion. *The Anatomy Lesson of Dr. van der Meer*, for example, painted by van Mierevelts in 1617, shows a group of men and their cadaver. The lighting is flat and the men stare out at the viewer without expression.

In characteristic fashion, Rembrandt painted *The Anatomy Lesson of Dr. Tulp* (1632) in a style unlike that of any other guild paintings. The impression it made on his patrons and the public bordered on sheer amazement. The pyramidal arrangement of the individuals takes it beyond the usual line of faces found in conventional group portraits. Only the two men at the back of the group peer out toward the viewer, enhancing the composition's physical depth. And the slightly diagonal position of the corpse emphasizes and changes the perspective.

Rembrandt's personal concept of realism is also evident. Anatomy dissections usually begin with an incision in the cadaver's abdomen. But Dr. Tulp is seen working on the hand while the rest of the cadaver is intact, emphasizing the importance of a physician's hands to his life's work. Rather than the usual naturalistic representation of an event found in other guild-commissioned portraits, Rembrandt's painting combines several themes at once, giving the picture a deeper significance while imbuing it with a notable sense of immediacy, movement, and spontaneity. These elements raise *The Anatomy Lesson of Dr. Tulp* out of the realms of mere decoration and bestow on it the formal dignity of an extraordinarily successful painting.

After *The Anatomy Lesson of Dr. Tulp* confirmed Rembrandt's reputation, he began an intense period of portrait painting, which gives a fascinating insight into the Dutch bourgeoisie of the times. He painted aristocrats and wealthy merchants, wives and families; married couples became a Rembrandt hallmark. In his portraits, he continued to capture the essential reality beneath each subject's superficial appearance. This is particularly evident in his portrait of Cornelius Anslo, in which the famous preacher is intently explaining a point of doctrine to a woman. It can also be seen in *The Shipbuilder and His Wife*, an extremely natural scene of family life that is singularly lacking in the usual stagnant and false adulation for the sitters that other commissioned portraits conveyed at this time.

Despite all his portrait work, Rembrandt did not neglect his religious and historical paintings. In 1634, Statholder Frederik Hendrik, a highly placed government official, bought two of these paintings—*The Raising of the Cross* and *The Deposition of Christ*. Hendrik was so pleased with his purchases that he ordered three more—*The Ascension*, *The Entombment*, and *The Resurrection*. These five paintings make up Rembrandt's famous *Passion* cycle, a great work of art imbued with powerful emotion. The scenes are impetuously full of movement. Some critics feel they show the distinct influence of Rubens's massive Baroque triptych in the Antwerp Cathedral completed ten years earlier. Certainly, the *Passion* cycle has a Baroque flavor, but the Statholder loved the Baroque style and Rembrandt's desire was to please his patron.

In the *Passion* cycle, however, the Baroque movement's mythical flourish, round, pink flesh, and idealistic swirls are subtle. All five paintings are pervaded with the realism Rembrandt so dearly loved. They all have the psychological scrutiny that is seldom lacking in his work. They all have his lavish attention to costume detail. Chiaroscuro is also brought to great new heights in these paintings. Every line seems to shimmer, imparting a remarkable and dramatic atmosphere to the images with not a trace of artifice.

Rembrandt was busy in these first few years in Amsterdam. And by 1634 he had achieved a good amount of wealth and fame.

It was the best of times to fall in love.

*The Blinding
of Samson*
(detail)

SASKIA

Rembrandt met Saskia at his art dealer's home. She was the beautiful twenty-two-year-old niece of Hendrick van Uylenburch. Her prominent Amsterdam family was wealthy, and Saskia brought him a veritable fortune as dowry when they married in July 1634.

Rembrandt loved her passionately and tenderly. Indeed, the early years of his marriage to Saskia were perhaps the happiest of his life. In 1639, he bought a fine house in the Breestraat section of Amsterdam. He did not have the money to pay for it all at once, but the future looked bright.

Rembrandt worked hard and life was not all light and fun, particularly since each of Saskia and Rembrandt's three children died in infancy. Then, in 1641, Saskia and Rembrandt's son Titus was born—and lived.

Rembrandt adored his son and frequently painted him. But Saskia was his favorite model. He painted her more than any other single person, leaving a lovely legacy of portraits. In *Portrait of Saskia with a Hat*, painted soon after their marriage, the young wife is dressed as a noblewoman. Rembrandt's insightful pictorial skills are further enriched by subtle traces of intimacy.

In *The Merry Couple* (1636), Saskia is sitting on the lap of a gentleman who can be clearly recognized as Rembrandt himself. The picture is a sparkling toast to the success and contentment the artist enjoyed at this time. Rich and famous, with no illusions about his considerable worth, Rembrandt painted himself in sumptuous clothing and in elegant surroundings. This painting has also been interpreted as a humorous response to Saskia's relatives, some of whom disapproved of their marriage. Rembrandt also painted Saskia as the goddess *Danaë*, as *Delilah*, as the exuberant *Flora*, in a continuous homage to her beauty and life.

Although it seemed as if all Rembrandt painted, all he thought about during the years between 1635 and 1642, was his beloved v ,ie, he did paint a great number of self-portraits and other works of astounding chromatic and conceptual impact. *Abraham's Sacrifice*, for example, is fraught with powerful emotion, its Baroque effusiveness tempered by skillful tonal illumination. *Susanna Surprised By the Elders*, a panel finished in 1637, demonstrates few of the qualities of a classic Grecian Venus. Instead, luminous against a brownish background, she displays Rembrandt's distinct taste for a more commonplace and real beauty. *Workers in the Vineyard*, with its extraordinary fusion of the figures with light, achieves a result of illustrative detail not unlike that in Rembrandt's etchings.

THE NIGHT WATCH

Sadly, the joys of wedded bliss were short-lived. In 1642, Saskia died. She was only thirty years old.

That same year, Rembrandt painted the most significant single picture of his career—*The Night Watch*.

When he began to work on his masterpiece, Rembrandt was no longer a joyous and contented man, enjoying a carefree and extravagant life in the company of his charming wife. He had lost two baby daughters and a baby son. His mother, for whom he had deep affection and love, had also died. And he had lost his beloved wife, the woman who was his inspiration.

Suddenly, Rembrandt was alone, rich and profoundly unhappy, left to care for his young son Titus. Despite his grief, or perhaps because of it, the masterpiece that was taking shape had signs of greatness. *The Night Watch* did not suffer along with its creator. It still involves and even overawes the viewer—as it must have done Captain Banning Cocq and the stalwart citizens of his company when they saw themselves for the first time immortalized on the large canvas they had commissioned.

The Night Watch, originally entitled *The Militia Company of Captain Banning Cocq*, depicts a group of civic guards, a platoon of musketeers. Until the canvas was cleaned in 1946, the dust and dirt that had accumulated over the centuries gave it a dark and shadowy aspect, almost obliterating some of the background figures. It seemed to take place in gloomy night, rather than in the daylight Rembrandt painted. Hence, in the nineteenth century the painting was named *The Night Watch*.

As with his earlier painting *The Anatomy Lesson of Dr. Tulp*, *The Night Watch* is nothing like other commissioned portraits of the day. There have certainly been great pictures of military patrols, such as those painted by Fans Hals (which are displayed in the Rijksmuseum of Amsterdam along with *The Night Watch*), but none have the unusual power of Rembrandt's masterpiece. Its most striking feature is its sense of participation and anticipation, its mystery. Something is obviously happening, but it is not at all certain what that something might be. The light glows almost from within the canvas, illuminating a young girl, a chicken dangling at her belt. A dog barks in a dark corner. A man bangs a wooden drum. The painting has an unsettling quality, as if it were about to move. The inexplicable action that is depicted is almost palatable. The spectator views the busy scene, the action that is projected from the canvas, and is both perplexed and fascinated. What does it mean?

Some claim the painting depicts a group of soldiers setting out to defend their city during the Siege of Amsterdam. Others say it shows a procession of civic guards during the visit of Maria de Medici in 1639. And, because each member of the company paid for the picture according to his prominence, it is difficult to tell who the protagonists are and who are merely incidental.

Rembrandt's great love of theater is confirmed in *The Night Watch*. The variety of figures and costumes, the movement that pervades the entire image, and the skillful use of lighting blend to suggest a very capable sense of scenic management. The mystery, too, is theater. A dramatic incident is being played out for eternity.

As is often the case with masterpieces, *The Night Watch* was not greeted with unanimous approval. Several of the members of the patrol were displeased at being portrayed in a scene of such dynamic action. They preferred the usual staid and orderly assembly. But Rembrandt's fame as an artist was not at all affected. Although it was controversial in Amsterdam circles, *The Night Watch* was still considered one of his most significant works.

Nevertheless, after *The Night Watch* was completed, Rembrandt began a new phase in his career, one that was more pensive and grave.

AMSTERDAM: THE SECOND PERIOD

Perhaps Rembrandt's spirit was still heavy in the years following *The Night Watch*. Certainly the self-portraits he painted around 1645 reflect a heavy spirit. The loss he had recently experienced, the heavy grief he still bore, the controversial reception of *The Night Watch*—all undoubtedly caused him to retreat into himself. He also had financial problems. He simply couldn't manage his personal affairs, especially the payments on his expensive Breestraat house. Fewer portraits were commissioned. Rembrandt became more particular about what he would take on. His former patrons sought the newest style: neoclassicist painting that looked for inspiration to the ancient worlds of Greece and Rome rather than to the Italian Renaissance.

Even more distressing was the drama unfolding in his private life. Rembrandt's longtime housekeeper, Geertje Dircx, grew jealous when, in 1649, he brought a pretty young peasant woman, Hendrickje Stoffels, into his household as a maid. Hendrickje soon gained the favors of her employer. She became Rembrandt's mistress and companion. Geertje left in a jealous rage and even took legal action against her employer. She claimed Rembrandt kept many valuables that really belonged to her.

Rembrandt was furious at what he considered a betrayal. The valuables in question were Saskia's, not Geertje's. Geertje sued for breach of promise—and won. Rembrandt was forced to pay her a monthly stipend at a time when he had little money. Geertje became unbalanced and while Rembrandt began a new life with Hendrickje, painting her tranquil expression in such works as *The Holy Family* and as *Flora*, Geertje grew worse. By the time Rembrandt and Hendrickje's daughter, Cornelia, was born in 1654, there was no going back for Geertje. She continued to bother Rembrandt, tormenting his waking hours. Eventually, goaded by anger and frustration, he paid the state to put her in an institution.

But Rembrandt's works during this period belie the turmoil in his personal life. His historical and biblical paintings evoked the masters of the past while remaining uniquely his own. The close links he had with the Amsterdam Jewish community gave him the opportunity to study in minute detail the ancient Semitic features. Combined with his thorough knowledge of the Bible, Rembrandt was able to paint religious paintings that were remarkable in their authenticity.

His new rendering of *Christ at Emmaus*, completed in 1648, is an excellent example. Here is the sense of exquisite detail, the exactness of features, the almost inner glow of light that mark Rembrandt's biblical pictures of this period. This painting is also characterized by Rembrandt's extreme equilibrium and composure that is evident during this period. Here, too, is the distinct influence of the masters of the Italian Renaissance. The overall composition is symmetrical; to avoid the impression of rigidity, Rembrandt shifted the viewpoint slightly to the left. The dynamic effects of his earlier *Christ at Emmaus* are replaced by an atmosphere of intimate and evocative participation.

Bathsheba, painted in 1654, continues to show Rembrandt's Italian influence—and his great equilibrium. Here, the play of light reaches exceptional levels; the firm and lively brushstrokes produce tender caresses, displaying Rembrandt's great technical expertise.

The Slaughtered Ox is only a small panel, but as a still-life composition it creates a monumental pictorial effect, turning the potentially trite genre into a supremely personal and grandiose interpretation that can stand alone.

A Woman Bathing (1654) displays the painterly techniques Rembrandt acquired during this period. His applications are softer, his brushstrokes more fluid, as if his compositions are created by light alone. The barely visible details of *Woman Bathing* stand out in the shape-inducing light only through brighter, more luminous highlights.

The etching of *Christ Healing*, painted about 1656, is an image filled with allusions and references testifying to the extent of Rembrandt's philosophical and religious knowledge. One of the disciples at the side of Jesus looks like Socrates. The faces of Erasmus and Descartes can also be seen. Rembrandt seems to suggest that religious contrast must be overcome.

Finally, there is *Jacob Blessing the Sons of Joseph*, which he painted in 1656. Like most of his other works of this period, Rembrandt demonstrated his preference for an atmosphere of intimacy and tranquillity. The complex interplay of hands, as Joseph attempts to shift the hands of the blind Jacob onto the head of his firstborn, show a dynamic but gentle passion, a tension between strength and vulnerability.

Rembrandt also painted landscapes during this period of serenity. He often sketched the canals around Amsterdam, walking

*Sampling
Officials of
the Drapers' Guild*
(detail)

along them as they left the city and entered the flat countryside, dotted by turning windmills and fields of grass. Stormy skies and prodigious ruins give way to more peaceful visions in such paintings as *Winter Landscape with Skaters* (1646). Here the dramatic elements of his earlier works are absent. The small figures are submerged in a delicately suspended atmosphere.

And, although he had fewer commissions, Rembrandt continued to do portraits. He painted friends and relatives, from Hendrickje to Titus. The portrait he did of his son in 1655 is touching in its sweetness and depth.

AMSTERDAM: THE THIRD PERIOD

In 1656, Rembrandt's financial state became so bad that he was forced to formally petition for *cessio bonorum* status: bankruptcy. All his possessions, his great works of art, his costumes, his silks and jewels, had to be auctioned to pay his creditors. Even his house had to be sold.

Luckily, Rembrandt avoided outright poverty because he was still the executor of the estate Saskia had left Titus and he still had all the income from that inheritance at his disposal. He signed over his income to Hendrickje and Titus at their insistence. Hendrickje wanted to manage his money and protect him from further debt. To that end, the small household moved to a modest home in a less elegant section of the city.

Although Rembrandt was now dependent on the support of his companion and his son, the years after 1660 were creative ones. He began moving toward a style that was free of academic limitations, free of public constraints. And, although he received little public support during his bankruptcy proceedings, Rembrandt continued to receive important commissions. In 1656, the year his finances were at their worst, he was commissioned to do *The Anatomy Lesson of Dr. Joan Deyman*, a work which unfortunately suffered serious damage in a fire.

And, in 1661-1662, Rembrandt painted his celebrated *Sampling Officials of the Drapers' Guild*. Once again, he endows the usually stagnant group portrait with a highly individual interpretation. The group is gathered around a table in the foreground, looking up and out at the viewer, at the "interruption" to their meeting.

27

The Conspiracy
of the Batavians
(detail)

The now mature Rembrandt obtains an outstanding realism and impact in this painting without resorting to spatial illusions or overworked textures of chiaroscuro. Instead, he creates an intense, absorbing composition with a simple horizontal arrangement and such skillfully placed elements as the red cloth over the table and the refined, subtle use of illumination.

Rembrandt also received an important order for *Conspiracy of the Batavians*, but, because of its decidedly "barbaric" feel, it was not appreciated by the people who paid for it. It was large and fraught with high drama. The swords and faces of the conspirators are daringly illuminated from below by the light reflected from the cloth on the table. It was different and highly realistic. Unfortunately, the commissioners had planned to hang the painting in Amsterdam's new town hall. They would have preferred a painting that had a bit more religious adulation. Rembrandt's accentuated realism was interpreted as a criticism of the emerging classicist school and it was rejected. In 1662, Rembrandt brought the painting back to his studio and cut it down.

Despite this debacle, Rembrandt continued to enjoy some prestige. Count Antonio Ruffo of Messina came to visit; he had purchased Rembrandt's *Aristotle Contemplating the Bust of Homer* and now he wanted two more paintings, *Alexander the Great* and *Homer*. Rembrandt painted them both between 1661 and 1663. These paintings show the mature artist's remarkable and vivacious style, although they are quite different in character. The count was not as pleased with the end result as Rembrandt would have hoped, but this could be because Rembrandt finished them much later than he had promised.

The third period of Rembrandt's career was characterized by isolation. Although he was still appreciated by an elite of connoisseurs, his popularity with the general public sharply declined. When Hendrickje died in 1663, he was deeply stricken. He felt more alone than ever.

But despite his grief and isolation, Rembrandt continued to paint great works of art. *The Bridal Couple*, one of his final triumphs, delineates an intimate scene of family life with skillful and confident strokes.

The mirthful expression depicted in *Self-Portrait Laughing*,

*Self-Portrait
Laughing*
(detail)

painted around 1665, seems to suggest a sardonic detachment from the painter's trials and tribulations.

In *The Family Group*, painted around 1668, Rembrandt emphasizes only the overall composition and the expressions on the family's faces. He effectively eliminated the unessential elements of the setting in a style that, several centuries later, would be emulated by many modern painters.

The Return of the Prodigal Son, also painted around 1668, has the mood of an abstract painting. The composition is dominated by a brilliant application of color that, in certain areas of the canvas, seems to be made of nothing but pure energy.

Before Rembrandt died on October 4, 1669, he had to face more grief. His son Titus died first, in 1668, at the age of twenty-seven.

Rembrandt's last painting was *Simeon Holding the Christ Child in the Temple*, which evokes the pain and sadness of his last years.

At the end of his long career, Rembrandt left a legacy of tremendous artistic output, including approximately seven hundred paintings and three hundred etchings. In his quest to seek out the soul beneath the surface, he used light, embracing it, embellishing it, and, ultimately, giving it a life of its own.

Soldier with Sword

Peter and Paul in Conversation

Peter and Paul in Conversation (detail)

Self-Portrait with Gorget

Soldier in a Plumed Hat

Scholar in Meditation

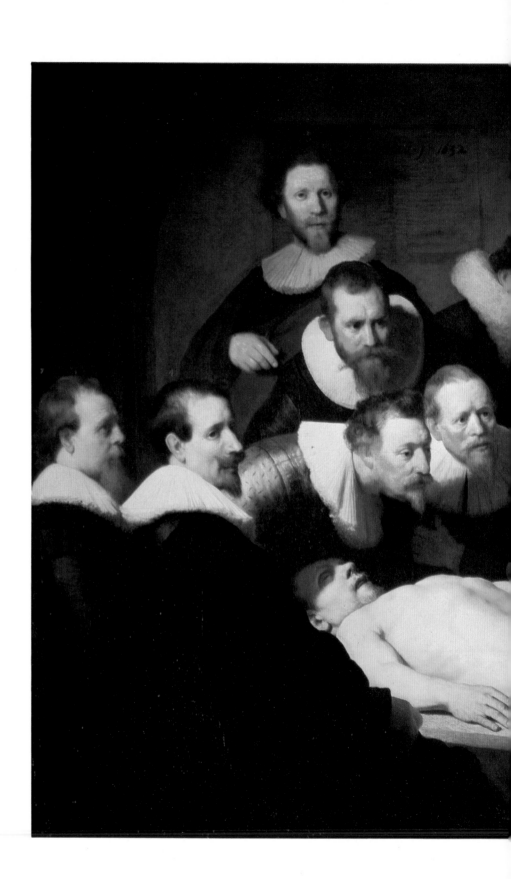

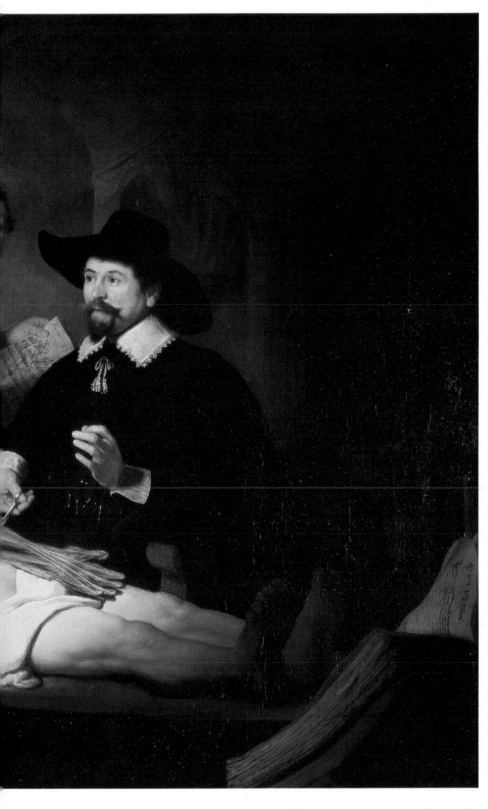

The Anatomy Lesson of Dr. Tulp

Saskia as Flora

The Descent from the Cross

Artemisia Receiving Her Husband's Ashes Mixed with Wine

Self-Portrait with Gorget and Beret

Rembrandt and Saskia in the Scene: The Prodigal Son in a Bordello

Female Figure with Laurel Crown

The Angel Preventing Abraham from Sacrificing His Son Isaac

The Angel Preventing Abraham from Sacrificing His Son Isaac (detail)

An Officer

Portrait of Saskia with a Hat

The Slaughtered Ox

The Holy Family

The Departure of the Sunamitic Woman

The Night Watch

The Night Watch (detail)

The Night Watch (detail)

Christ and the Woman Taken in Adultery

Christ and the Woman Taken in Adultery (detail)

The Adoration of the Shepherds

Abraham Serving the Three Angels

Winter Landscape with Skaters

Susannah Surprised by the Elders

Susannah Surprised by the Elders (detail)

Christ at Emmaus

Christ at Emmaus (detail)

Sarah Waiting for Tobias

Danaë, or Aegina Visited by Jupiter in the Form of Fire

Portrait of a Bareheaded Man

The Flight into Egypt

Portrait of an Old Woman in a Veil

A Woman Bathing

An Old Woman Reading

Portrait of Catrina Hooghsaet

The Man with the Golden Helmet

The Man with the Golden Helmet (detail)

Jacob Blessing the Sons of Joseph

Moses with the Tablets of the Law

Two Negroes

Alexander the Great

Alexander the Great (detail)

Homer

The Suicide of Lucretia

Haman Recognizes His Fate

Haman Recognizes His Fate (detail)

The Return of the Prodigal Son

Simeon's Song of Praise

Self-Portrait

Stampa Grafiche Editoriali Padane Cremona